Jesse Helms and the Legacy of Nathaniel Macon

by
Ronnie W. Faulkner

**Jesse Helms
and the
Legacy
of Nathaniel
Macon**
©1998 The Jesse Helms Center
Wingate, North Carolina 28174

The Jesse Helms Center
P.O. Box 247
3918 U.S. Highway 74 East
Wingate, North Carolina 28174
704-233-1776

Past things shed light on future ones. The
world was always of a kind. What is and will
be was at some other time. The same things
keep coming back, but under different names
and colors. Not everybody recognizes them but
only he who is wise and considers them diligently.

Francesco Guicciardini (1482-1540)

"Always of a Kind"

Upon elevation of a Tar Heel senator to the chairmanship of the Committee on Foreign Relations, a disgruntled president wrote that the man was characterized by "a narrowness of mind which education cannot enlarge, and covered by an encrustation of prejudices which experience cannot remove."[1] Congressman Charles J. Ingersoll wrote of the same senator: "Negation was his ward and arm.... No ten members [of Congress] gave so many negative votes."[2] Still others, examining critically his long career, were quick to label him "a demagogue,"[3] "a negative radical,"[4] and a man "of mediocre abilities and meager education, ... erring more often in his grammar than in his moral principles."[5]

The man who was the target of these criticisms was not Republican Senator Jesse Helms, though the philosophy and tactics of the person so assailed--Senator Nathaniel Macon--closely parallels Helms in almost every particular. Most senators lack historic memory when they attempt to explain Helms. As Ernest B. Furgurson wrote in his book on the senator:

> Repeatedly, as they speak of Helms, other senators
> and political veterans refer back to the way things
> used to be, the old days, the institution and its
> traditions. Helms puzzles them when they look for a

political mold into which he fits, another historic
figure with whom he compares.[6]

Then Furgurson wanders into strained comparisons with George C. Wallace and Joseph R. McCarthy. Another analyst, Elizabeth Drew of the New Yorker wrote of Helms with seeming prescience: "The substance of his politics is... a throwback to an old streak in American political life."[7] She proceeds to disappoint by an exposition on the racial overtones of the Frank Porter Graham-Willis Smith senate campaign of 1950 in which Helms played a minor part.

Sociologist Paul Luebke comes closer to the truth in Tar Heel Politics: Myths and Realities (1990) wherein he sees Helms as representing a form of "traditionalism" which emerged from "the culture of North Carolina's small towns and rural areas."[8] Traditionalism, he maintains, is religiously fundamentalist, free enterprise-oriented, anti-tax, and anti-big government. But Luebke deals primarily with the twentieth century, connecting the group to the state's capitalist elite, and failing to delve into traditionalism's ultimate roots.[9]

The true origin of the Helms phenomenon goes back well beyond this century--to the pre-capitalist, agrarian foundations of the Republic and to North Carolina's first major political leader--Nathaniel Macon. Like Helms, Macon hailed from a rural environment about which he often waxed nostalgic. Like Helms, he fought a centralized federal government. And also like Helms, Macon was both religiously devout and an admirer of Thomas Jefferson. Biographer Stephen J. Barry has written of Macon: "His brand of plain republicanism had its origin in the distinct political culture of the North Carolina backcountry."[10]

Macon's republicanism derived in large part from Anti-Federalism. Anti-Federalism in the 1780s represented the well-established American tradition of decentralized government and local autonomy and hence was more "conservative" than the opposing force of Federalism, which advocated stronger central government. That the Federalists were politically savvy is revealed by their co-option of the very name that implied the opposite of what they were: The Federalists were "radical" and "nationalist," while the Anti-Federalists were "conservative" and "federalist." Of the two parties that emerged from this early conflict--the Federalists and the Republicans--only the later had a lasting influence on North Carolina.[11]

Macon was, during the early years of the Republic, the embodiment of Tar Heel republicanism, both politically and religiously. On the religious side, he not only attended Baptist services regularly, but impressed Thomas Hart Benton of Missouri as "deeply imbued with Bible images" and as "a pious and religious man."[12] Barry has noted that Macon early in his life "underwent a pronounced religious conversion."[13] Helms, perhaps feeling a spiritual kinship with Macon, once visited the isolated grave of the old Republican and vowed the preservation of the home and grave of "this great man who is now all but forgotten." At another point he wrote that "[Macon] and his amazing career are evidence aplenty of the worthiness of limited government."[14]

Macon was born in what is now Warren County on December 17, 1758, to a planter family. In the 1770s he briefly attended the College of New Jersey (Princeton).[15] Macon never finished his formal studies. He left school to serve as a soldier in the Revolution, first in 1776 in the New Jersey militia and in 1780-81 in the North Carolina militia. He left the military when elected a state senator. As a politician, Macon was an early opponent of adoption of the Constitution. Yet, once North Carolina approved the Constitution, he became a proponent of "strict construction" and limited government--a Jeffersonian Republican. "He believed that government was inherently corrupt," wrote his most recent biographer. "And he was convinced that the extent of this corruption was proportional to the size of government."[16]

In 1791 he entered Congress, serving as Speaker of the House during the administration of Jefferson, a personal friend. He was elected to the U.S. Senate in 1815 and served there until his retirement in 1828, having reached "three-score years and ten."[17] He returned to his modest 16 x 20 foot plantation house[18] and told John Randolph, his best friend in Congress, that he "never once regretted" leaving public life.[19] Macon died at home on June 29, 1837, surrounded by friends and slaves. A modest planter, he was neither ostentatious nor materialistic, being very much like the "plain folk" described by Frank L. Owsley in his seminal 1949 work <u>Plain Folk of the Old South</u>.[20] Product of a patriarchal society, he shared the views and tastes of the common folk who continually returned him to office.

Macon's twentieth century incarnation, Jesse Helms, was born in Monroe, Union County, on October 18, 1921, the son of a police chief. He attended both Wingate Junior College and Wake Forest College, but like Macon did not finish his studies. Interestingly, those who remember him from his college days do not recall him as being political, but remember "a clean-living Baptist."[21] For a while he worked part-time for the <u>News and Observer</u>, then as a reporter for the <u>Raleigh Times</u>.

Helms's patriotic inclination is revealed by his enlistment in the navy in World War II, serving from 1942 to 1945. After the war, he became involved in politics, briefly working on the staffs of Democratic Senators Willis Smith and Alton Lennon, 1951-53. Thereafter, he became executive director of the North Carolina Bankers Association and gained notice as editor of the organization's newsletter. Helms went on to serve as news and program director for WRAL radio and later as executive vice-president of Capitol Broadcasting Company, operators of WRAL-TV and WRAL radio. For over twelve years, from 1960 to 1972, he was the editorial voice of WRAL's nightly Viewpoint Editorial. No man's views were better known to Tar Heels than his when he was elected to the U.S. Senate in 1972.[22]

In the intervening years Helms has been continually returned to the Senate. He has been popular on both ends of the economic spectrum--with businessmen because of his laissez-faire economic philosophy and with blue-collar workers because of his social conservatism.[23] In this, as in other areas, Helms's career closely mirrors that of Macon.

The Bible and Good Government

In 1831 the Frenchman Alexis de Tocqueville observed that family stability inherent in America's Christian faith carried over into the political and social spheres. "While the law allows the American people to do everything," wrote Tocqueville, "there are things which religion prevents them from imagining and forbids them to dare." As evidence, the French observer related a court incident in New York state where a judge dismissed a witness who professed atheism "on the ground that the witness had destroyed beforehand all possible confidence in his testimony."[24]

At that same time, 1831, former Senator Macon, who attended a church near his Buck Spring home and professed to be of "the Baptist persuasion," gathered his seventy some slaves in front of his house every Sunday to read to them from Scripture.[25] One historian wrote that Macon's "favorite literature was the Bible, and his austere and pure character is an argument stronger than words that he never imbibed the dregs of the skeptical Illuminati."[26] For him the Holy Book was a guide for both the individual and society:

> The whole Bible contains great knowledge of the
> principles of government. The rising generations
> forget the principles and maxims of their forefathers;
> hence the destruction of free government in every age.
> Of what benefit was the law to the children of Israel
> when they departed from it, or what benefit are
> written constitutions if they be departed from?[27]

Seeing the enlargement of government through protectionism, taxes, and internal improvements, Macon told Bartlett Yancey that "the book of Judges ought to be attentively read by every man in the United States to see the terrible effect on the Israelites for departing from the law..."[28]

In the Book of Judges, after the death of Joshua, who led the Jews in their military victories in the Promised Land, the children of Israel ignored their spiritual obligations. In 2:12 it says: "And they forsook the Lord God of their fathers, which brought them out of the land of Egypt, and followed other gods, of the gods of the people that were round about them, and bowed themselves unto them, and provoked the Lord to anger."

When Congress moved to repeal the Embargo Act in 1809 without any resolution of the conflict with Great Britain, Macon cried: "The Lord, the Mighty Lord, must come to our assistance or I fear we are undone as a nation."[29] In 1818 he advised a friend "in fear of God, and for love of the Constitution" to "add not to the Constitution nor take therefrom.... Remember you belong to a meek State and just people who want nothing but to enjoy the fruits of their labor honestly and to lay out their profits in their own way."[30] Josephus Daniels, newspaperman and Wilson administration official, correctly noted that Macon was guided by two documents: the Constitution and the Bible.

Indeed, Macon came to adhere as strictly to the letter of the Constitution, which he termed a "sacred instrument," as he did the words of the Good Book.[31]

Notably, Jesse Helms, an active Baptist, a deacon, and former Sunday School teacher, is guided by the same documents. He often cites the same book of the Bible and even the same verses in illustrating his points, revealing thereby a clear congruence with the thinking of Macon. A reporter from the News and Observer has written: "To know what motivates Helms is to understand what lessons he draws from the Bible."[32] In his 1976 book, When Free Men Shall Stand, Helms wrote in the first sentence of chapter one: "The situation in our country today is remarkably similar to that of Israel in the days of the Judges." He then adds:

> Spiritually we know we are all Israel, for Christ
> teaches that God's admonitions and promises to Israel
> will be fulfilled also in the New Testament times and
> peoples. In the brief history of our own country
> since we gained our independence, we can look back
> upon a tremendous heritage of political freedom
> founded upon a biblical faith.... The all-provident
> Government...is the modern day version of Baal....[33]

From the above examples it is obvious that Macon and Helms shared a similar religious perspective that impacted their politics, leading to both philosophical and operational similarities between the two men. But first, we should review the related question of the separation of church and state as practiced and understood in Macon's day.

Church
and
State

      The issue of church and state is bound up with the original conception that states had a right to do things prohibited to the central government. In the debate over the Alien and Sedition Acts, Macon said that the law threatened not only free speech and the press, but opened the door for establishment of religion. He suggested that the states had a right to punish sedition, but not the Congress which "ought to have confidence in the States."[34]

      From 1776 to 1835 the Constitution of North Carolina, under which Macon lived, held that "no person who shall deny the being of God, or the truth of the Protestant religion, or the divine authority of the Old or New Testaments, ... shall be capable of holding any office, or place of trust or profit, in the civil department, within this State." The same 1776 Constitution also maintained that "there shall be no establishment of any one religious church or denomination in this state," demonstrating that establishment was interpreted in a narrow constitutional light.[35]

      While Macon believed the Bible a valuable guide for governance, he did not believe in theocracy. As president of the 1835 state Constitutional Convention, he opposed any religious test for office and maintained that "a mixture of Politics and Religion was the very essence of hypocrisy." As to the question of debarring atheists from office, Macon declared that he "did not believe there ever was an atheist, whatever his nation or color."[36] In other words, why have a test for something that was merely theoretical?

Macon's argument in the case of the Alien and Sedition Acts proved that he viewed the religious provision of the Constitution as a state matter. The wording of the religious provision was changed from "Protestant" to "Christian" in 1835 and again after northern victory in the Civil War. Nonetheless, even the imposed Constitution of 1868 prohibited atheists from holding office.[37] While these things transpired, North Carolina's largest denomination, the Baptists, to which Macon claimed allegiance, raised no particular objections.

The above facts are important because they belie the mistaken belief that the First Amendment embodies an anti-clericalism similar to that of the French Revolution. At the same time, they reveal that separation of church and state was not absolutist in Macon's time. The prohibition on establishment of religion was a restriction only on the federal government, but prayer and religious ceremonies on public occasions were not only not prohibited but were protected by the separation of powers within the federal system between the nation and the states.

Helms's, who has a Macon-type view of religious issues, traces American liberty not to the Enlightenment, but through "centuries of Christian teaching." In 1976 he wrote: "Ultimately, the author of human liberty is almighty God, who endows each human being with free will.... We must turn to the Author of Liberty to enjoy again what once we had so abundantly."[38]

Helms's basic conception of America as a religious nation has been defended by historian M. E. Bradford in his 1993 book Original Intentions, where the author devotes a chapter to an analysis of the religious convictions of about 150 Founders, not just the few deists who get inordinate attention from modern scholars. He concluded from evidence that the typical Founder was "a conventional Christian and social conservative."[39] Though Helms is not credited, the Helmsian outlook was expounded on at length by M. Stanton Evans in his 1994 book The Theme is Freedom: Religion, Politics, and the American Tradition. Evans argues that the Western concepts of political freedom and limited government "come to us from the religion of the Bible."[40] More recently, Judge Robert Bork argued in <u>Slouching Towards Gomorrah</u> (1996) for the value of traditional religion in preserving and revitalizing American democratic culture.[41]

To the above sentiments both Macon and Helms could agree without any predisposition to <u>legally</u> require a certain set of religious beliefs. The simple acknowledgment that our political institutions have religious roots is not to say that America has ever been a theocracy. However, it is safe to postulate that a knowledge of faith may better inform one's political decisions.

Governmental Consolidation and Broad Construction

Macon believed that the genius of the American system was revealed by a Constitution which limited the actions of the central government by enumerating powers and reserving most rights to the people and the states. He feared the expansion of the welfare clause which might make the federal government "unlimitted [sic] by degrees."[42] "In giving a stretching construction to the Constitution," he said in 1820, "we ought not to forget the Holy Scripture, which was, by a stretching construction, made to cover a terrible inquisition and wild crusades."[43]

Macon distrusted precedent, fearing that an unconstitutional action could easily become a precedent for further dubious acts. He said: "I am willing to execute the Constitution just as it was understood by those who made it, and no other."[44] This is what we today call the doctrine of original intent or understanding and is promoted by Robert Bork and others.

Some might argue that Macon, who knew the framers, had a more creditable claim to understanding "original intent" than modern theorists. In truth, however, there is a wealth of evidence in the documentation of the federal convention and the state ratification conventions to give any jurist a substantive basis for interpretation based on intent. As Bork has noted, if one cannot reasonably rule from original meaning, then a written Constitution serves no true purpose.[45]

The above basic attitudes are shared by Helms. Giving a speech in London in 1973, Helms said in speaking of the American Constitution: "Our particular contribution was the philosophical development of the concept of limited powers." He also wrote in 1976: "The great aim of our republic, the concept that distinguished it from all the countries of the old world, was preventing the consolidation of political power." Helms, like Macon, has a fear of unconstitutional precedent and believes in Constitutional interpretation based on original intent. In the case of school prayer, as in many other cases, he has concluded that "the Court forced from the Constitution exactly the opposite conclusion from what the founding fathers intended."[46]

The Supreme Court

Though Macon was an early supporter of judicial review, he did not believe the Charles Evans Hughes dictum that "the Constitution is what the judges say it is."[47]   In fact, speaking for repeal of the Judiciary Act in 1802, Macon said that it was "extremely dangerous to the rights of the people for any person not elected by them to undertake to exercise the power of legislating for them.... Judges have no powers but what are given by the Constitution or by statute." Macon ridiculed the idea that the people's representatives could not act "because judges do not agree with us in political opinion."[48] After the 1803 case of Marbury vs. Madison, Macon wrote:

> The court must make every declaration of the unconstitutionality
> of a law at their peril; because the judges
> are made accountable for their conduct by the Constitu-
> tion, & if judges could declare acts void without being
> liable for their actions, they would be the supreme
> authority of the nation, and that without controul [sic] -and
> the only department in the Government where power might
> be exercised to any degree, without the least check or
> controul [sic] by any other department of the Government.[49]

Thomas Jefferson himself told Macon in 1821 that the courts needed to be controlled. He warned the Senator that "the engine of consolidation will be the Federal judiciary."[50] Macon believed that jurists should practice the restraint of narrow construction and original intent. If they did not, then he felt the people had a remedy through their elected representatives, who could abolish lower federal courts and reform the Supreme Court. After all, Congress represented the people and was the superior branch of government. Macon vigorously opposed "political authority of the judiciary."[51]

Senator Helms's attitudes toward the Supreme Court share much with Macon. Almost thirty years ago Helms condemned a Supreme Court "which for nearly two decades has been legislating instead of adjudicating."[52] He has long maintained that Congress could, by use of its powers under Article III, Section 2, control or prohibit court actions by limiting federal court appellate jurisdiction "with such Exceptions and under such Regulations as the Congress shall make." His battle for school prayer is a case in point: "My school prayer bill states simply that the federal courts shall not have jurisdiction, decree, or order denying or restricting as unconstitutional, voluntary prayer in any public school." At the same time Helms states that "no individual should be forced to participate in a religious exercise that is contrary to his or her religious convictions."[53] Under the Helms proposal only state courts would have jurisdiction.

In opposing the Helms interpretation, a great deal is often made of the Senator's lack of a law degree, ignoring the fact that the Constitution was not designed for the sole interpretation of lawyers. In the final analysis, as the previous discussion of church and state reveals, Helms's view closely approximates that which prevailed in the early years of the Republic.[54]

Taxes and Debt

Macon told William H. Crawford on October 13, 1817: "Our strength is in proportion to the smallness of our taxes; encumber and overload us with debt, and we are ruined."[55] In 1824 Macon observed that many men were offering themselves to the people for president. "Why, when I go home," he said, "they will ask me whom I think to be the best man; or rather, who will tax them the least? which is the same thing."[56] This attitude was a primary reason Macon generally opposed taxes and spending.

It was indeed fitting that Macon's first successful legislation was a tax reduction. In 1796 a crop failure resulted in decreased whiskey production among farmers in Warren County. Macon introduced a resolution replacing the annual excise tax on still capacity with a tax on the quantity of whiskey produced. A bill passed allowing the farmers to pay a tax of 10 cents per gallon for the time the still was in use, as against the annual 54 cents per gallon of capacity.[57]

In 1792 Nathaniel Greene's widow appealed for payment of $60,000 in army debts upon which Greene had acted as surety.   Macon voted against the measure, which nonetheless passed. In 1793-94, Macon was almost alone in opposing a grant of $4000 to the daughters of the French Count de Grasse, commander of the French fleet at Yorktown. "On the very day when we have come to a resolution to receive no more petitions from our fellow citizens," Macon protested, "we are going to give at once so large a sum to foreigners."[58] The grant was approved.

Even when Macon's personal friend, Thomas Jefferson, would benefit from governmental largesse, Macon said, "No!". He voted against the purchase of Jefferson's library in 1815. In 1824, after a triumphal tour, Marquis de Lafayette's friends in Congress proposed awarding him $200,000 and 24,000 acres of land. Macon protested: "Many native Americans spent their all, made great sacrifices, and devoted their lives to the same cause." Again he was outvoted, this time by a margin of 37 to 7.[59]

Macon voted for revenue measures only under the most dire circumstances, such as in cases of war. He otherwise argued that taxes were self-defeating because the great bulk of the freemen bore the tax burden regardless where along the economic ladder the tax was levied. In 1806, he correctly noted that to a businessman a tax was a part of his cost: "The consumer not only pays all the tax and charges on merchandise, but he pays them, with a profit to the merchant."[60]

Macon also believed that a personal predisposition toward indebtedness reflected a moral weakness that made one less mindful of the public purse. To him debt was "this great evil, which affects the moral as much as it does the political world."[61] In 1800 he said the country should pay its debts and "not leave it to our children."[62] He was doubtless thinking of Henry Clay's indebtedness when he wrote: "The rulers of a nation ought not to be in debt.... Whether in public or private life, those in debt, are generally projectors, under the hope that every new project may afford them some relief or make them rich."[63]

Macon was frugal, both personally and with public money. He refused pay for military service and never adopted the common practice of charging double mileage for travel while a senator. He opposed the franking privilege and declined payment as president of the state Constitutional Convention of 1835. Not surprisingly, whenever anyone introduced any salary increase for government workers, Macon inevitably opposed the raise. In fact, in 1795 he fought successfully for a reduction of the per diem for members of Congress from $7 to $6. He was one of the small minority opposed to a set salary of $1500 a year for Congressmen in 1816, and did not have to back peddle as did his colleagues when public outrage brought about prompt repeal.[64]

The example of Macon's economy has clearly impacted Helms, who said of Macon in 1982: "His unfailing efforts in behalf of frugality of public expenditures should be an inspiration to us all."[65] Helms has more consistently condemned "the dangerous and immoral practice of deficit spending" than any other member of Congress. "This is nothing but borrowing against the futures of our children and grandchildren," he warned. He has similarly noted: "Nothing comes easier than spending public money."[66] The senator has likewise proposed a flat tax, arguing as did Macon that individuals pay all taxes and that "there really is no such thing as a tax on business."[67]

To avoid the pitfall of over spending, Senator Helms has year after year returned a portion of his allocated office budget to the United States Treasury, totaling over $3 million. He has consistently been the most frugal member of Congress, never taking junkets and never mass mailing at taxpayer expense, sharing Macon's distaste for the franking privilege. Finally, he has taken steps virtually unheard of in Washington, such as his proposal to return portions of his salary for missing Senate work days while campaigning for others.[68] These actions reveal a Macon-style stewardship of public funds.

Legislation and Tyranny

It should come as no great shock, given Macon's attitudes, that he was not enamored of passing laws. Noting this, one historian who admired Macon nonetheless wrote that he "was not what would then or now be called a progressive or constructive statesman."[69] Macon has suffered from the predisposition to rate legislators as successful based upon bills that they get passed, even though it can be plausibly argued that the role of opposing legislation is equally important.

On the floor of Congress in 1806 Macon declared: "I am not of the opinion that it is sound policy to pass laws as fast as we can. On the contrary, I believe the less legislation the better." During the debate over slavery in 1820 Macon said: "The attempt to govern too much has produced every civil war that ever has been, and will, probably, every one that ever may be."[70]

In 1802 Macon spoke for repeal of the lame-duck Federalist Judiciary Act. One clever Federalist legislator, using a popular modern argument, declared that repeal would weaken the legal avenues for the poor and lead to their oppression. Understanding that governmental power in any form is always subject to elite manipulation, Macon responded: "Nothing but too much law can anywhere put it in the power of the rich to oppress the poor."[71]

Macon was against "governing too much," especially from Washington as it gradually came under the thrall of abolitionism. He started his career as a typically conflicted Jeffersonian on the issue of slavery, which he termed "a misfortune... a curse... an evil which our forefathers had felt, and to which we must submit until an adequate cure was found."[72]

When some called slavery "morally wrong" during the Missouri Compromise debate in 1820, however, Macon shifted to a more bucolic view. He said Northern Senators needed to go home with Southern Senators and "witness the meeting between slaves and the owner, and see the glad faces and the hearty shaking of hands." He especially spoke of the care and respect given old servants. Macon has been criticized for slipping into "sinister extravagances" to defend slavery.[73] Nonetheless, there is evidence that Macon displayed concern for the health of his slaves. Writing Randolph on April 26, 1829, the former senator indicated that many were sick and added that he would visit his very best friend, who was also ill, "as soon as I can leave with propriety my sick Negroes."[74]

Macon, as a Southern planter, well understood the source of freedom and slavery. "Let a man depend upon himself and he is free," he said in 1824. "If he is dependent on another, black or white, he will not be free."[75] To Macon an overpowering and centralized government trying to legislate every aspect of the citizens lives was the paramount threat to freedom. This is why Macon, while in Congress, "hardly ever proposed any measure."[76] The less legislation, the less government, the more liberty.

Indeed, Senator Helms in his "sobering look at the supertaxing, superspending, superbureaucracy in Washington," wrote of liberals: "Their creed and their platforms call for the enactment of ever more laws."[77] Helms, like Macon, has made a specialty not out of proposing legislation, but by fighting to stop legislation. His efforts have earned him the distinction of being called "Senator No" by the Raleigh News and Observer.[78] Senator Helms has reveled in this oppositional role, even comparing it in 1998 to the role played by Nathaniel Macon, "the original Senator No." Helms said:

"When it comes to saying 'no,' I am not in the same ballpark with Senator Macon, who was a fierce opponent of any and all measures to expand the power of the new federal government."[79]

Hard Money

One of Macon's most salient beliefs was in the efficacy of "hard money"--the belief that all money should have intrinsic value. "No man is more opposed to paper money than I am," he told Congress.[80] From retirement, Macon wrote Martin Van Buren: "The U.S. constitution was made for hard money, all paper or rag money is the same, whether called bank bills or paper money, it is too easy made & a part of all people are willing to have it because it is as easy got as made, though not worth much it will pay debts."[81]

The speculative aspect of the "American System," as advocated by Henry Clay and fulfilled by the Bank of the United States' issuance of paper money was not lost on Macon. The combination of the commercial interests with the government was a corrupting influence on every aspect of governance. The South, as an agricultural region, was especially hard hit by the evils Macon saw in the paper system--devalued currency, economic panic, and the reliance of speculators on the unholy bank-government coalition.[82]

Senator Helms has long advocated the modern version of the "hard" money tradition by supporting the gold standard. The senator, with Phil Crane, sponsored a law allowing American citizens gold ownership in 1974. He played a key role in the establishment of the U.S. Gold Commission, which he co-founded with Congressman Ron Paul.[83]

In his book, <u>When Free Men Shall Stand</u>, Helms states: "We should now start laying the foundation for genuine and enduring prosperity by insisting on a return to 'hard' money." After explaining how this is in line with the commandment "Thou shalt not steal," he declares that the United States "should reinstitute the backing of our money with precious metals." Why? He holds that it would stabilize the currency, impose discipline on public spending, and above all "would make our currency independent of political manipulation and chicanery."[84]

Free Enterprise and Government

Governmental plans that interfered with business were not to Macon's liking. When a petition of Nicholas J. Roosevelt and Jacob Mark asking for protection of their mining and manufacturing interests was reported favorably from committee in 1797, Macon said that "the best policy... in all such cases is to leave the business to the industry of our citizens.... They would work the mines if it was their interest to do so; if not, he did not want to offer them an inducement to do it."[85] In 1817 Macon, opposing internal improvements, argued that such things should be left to the industry of individuals and not to the government.[86]

Macon was a free trader. He opposed embargoes against France under the Federalists and was one of the last holdouts in the movement to embargo British goods under Republican administrations. He gave a speech on March 10 and 11, 1806, in opposition to a proposed embargo of tobacco and cotton shipments to England because it would "operate excessively hard on one part of the Union." He argued: "Adopt general measures, which will operate equally in every part of the country, and if the shoe is to pinch, let it pinch all alike, and all will be willing to have it off as soon as possible." He pronounced the dictum: "Trade thrives best when left to itself."[87]

Almost twenty years later Macon wrote Jefferson:

> The acts of the banks of the United States, the
> tariff and internal improvements seem to have put an
> end to legislating on the old republican principles,
> and to prove, that under any party name, unconstitu-
> tional measures may be adopted.... The acts above
> mentioned and such as may be expected to follow tend I
> fear, to make Congress bargainers and traders than
> sound and fair legislators; to look forward, cannot be
> pleasing, especially to those who have been opposed to
> constructive & implied powers in the federal government.[88]

"In all countries," wrote Macon, "those who have sense enough to get and keep money may be safely trusted as to the manner of disbursing it."[89] Such sentiments as this led one Congressman to note that Macon had no sense of public charity and "kept the public purse more stingily than his own."[90] Yet it would be a mistake to say that the senator did not value private charity, for as Benton said of him: "He never subscribed to charities, but gave, freely, according to his means."[91]

Senator Helms's views on free enterprise and charity are similar. He has argued: "No product and no man's labor ought to be artificially propped or protected in price."[92] Not surprisingly, Helms opposed the $3.5 billion Chrysler bailout and similar aid to business. He has also opposed the minimum wage and manifests a strong anti-union sentiment, both stands in keeping with his state's "Right to Work" tradition. Many critics have noted, not without reason, that Helms's support of federal tobacco programs is not consistent with his overall free enterprise position. Yet, no prominent Tar Heel politician has ever opposed tobacco. Being from the nation's leading tobacco-producing state does make a difference. But even with tobacco Helms has been prone toward federal deregulation.[93]

As to charity, Helms, like Macon, does not believe in public charity and has stated: "Nowhere and at no time, did Christ mention a government welfare program, let alone endorse one. He suggested another way, one that would work." He also has cited Davy Crockett: "We have the right, as individuals, to give away as much of our own money as we please to charity; but as members of Congress we have no right to appropriate even one dollar of the public money (for such a purpose)."[94]

Helms believes in the Biblical teaching of 2 Corinthians 9:7, "Every man according as he purposeth in his heart, so let him give; not grudgingly, or of necessity: for God loveth a cheerful giver." The senator is one of the few public officials who appreciates the difference between contributing one's own resources to charity, as he has done in the case of the fight against cerebral palsy, and foisting that responsibility off on the taxpayers. This baffles critics who contrast his "weak spot" for personal giving with his "coldly cruel" attitude toward government largesse.[95] This lack of comprehension reveals more about the senator's opponents than it does about Helms.

Principles
and
Party

     "It has been my lot to differ in some things with every administration," Macon told Andrew Jackson during the nullification controversy.[96] Indeed, regardless the party in power Macon ranked his consistent philosophy above party loyalty. "Principles can never change," he wrote in 1824, "and what has lately been called the law of circumstances is an abandonment of principle, and has been the ruin of all free governments, and if the Republican party fall in the United States, it is owing to the same cause."[97]

     Because of his firm attachment to principle Macon started to use tactics in the Federalist Congress of the 1790s that were to become characteristic of his career. As historian James M. Helms, Jr. pointed out, Macon made "a determined attack on the whole Federalist program, defeating what he could, obstructing by parliamentary maneuver what he could not defeat, and amending into uselessness what he could not otherwise obstruct."[98]

     As a member of the House under Federalist control in 1794, Macon introduced a series of resolutions to extend the unpopular whiskey excise tax to other alcohol products. Macon, who opposed the tax, was trying to extend the burden to every portion of the country. As one biographer wrote, Macon understood "the Hamiltonians were strong enough to prevent any such measure from passing, yet he was asking the

House to declare itself on the 'clear principle of justice.'" The proposal was rejected by a large margin, but the Federalists were forced to go on record favoring an injustice against the rural distillers of whiskey.[99]

Macon and the Southern Republicans were often charged with demagogic appeals, obstructionism, and working for the destruction of the government. On February 28, 1798, Macon responded. He noted "that both sides" appealed to the galleries in speeches. He indicated that the South "would most probably, in any convulsion, be the greatest losers.... Some gentlemen had charged them with wishing to stop the wheels of Government, whilst others had spoken of them as wishing to add a fifth wheel." Why was this? Because, he said, the Southerners "had not been the promoters of banks, funding and excise systems, stamp acts, etc."[100] A frustrated Connecticut Congressman, responding to Macon's tactics, said that his constituents would compel action. Macon "assure[d] the gentleman he would not be compelled to act."[101]

A month later Macon introduced a resolution to further delay retaliation against France by making any action apply also to Britain and Spain. Furious Federalists attacked him for being hypocritical, "blind" to U.S. interests, and inconsistent. He defended himself vigorously, and was called down by the Speaker for suggesting that no one east of Delaware fought in the South during the Revolution and that the South should be left alone.[102]

After the Republican victory in 1800, one might expect that the new Speaker would be more inclined toward party loyalty, or at least loyalty to the newly elected president. Jefferson, as a practical politician and a product of the Enlightenment, could change principles and shift positions in order to achieve his legitimate ends. But as one scholar wrote: "Macon, on the other hand, became so stubbornly attached to his postulates, once arrived at, that nothing short of a direct order from Heaven could detach him from them."[103] Macon quickly proved that he was no party man, even objecting to the unsuccessful attempt by his party to impeach Supreme Court Justice Samuel Chase because of the latter's political pronouncements from the bench.[104]

Then again, on issues of war and peace, Macon showed no more enthusiasm in building up the peace time military against Britain than he had against France. He objected to spending $150,000 in January of 1806 to improve coastal fortifications. When a fellow Republican pointed out that this was recommended by Jefferson, Macon responded: "I am not sent here to obey his mandates, or carry into effect what he recommends; but to obey the judgment which God gave me, and that I shall do whoever is President."[105] When his party balked at his delaying tactics, Macon said: "It is always better to decide rightly than quickly."[106]

Once an embargo was adopted Macon believed the country was morally obligated to stand by it until the British gave satisfaction. When this failed, Macon became an advocate of military action. Favoring no halfway measures, he proposed to enroll 20,000 troops for five-year terms to show that America meant business. Throughout the War of 1812, Macon, known to oppose taxes and expenditures, voted generous sums to prosecute the war. In this, as in most things, Macon was consistent. He argued against standing armies and large military expenditures in time of peace, but in war he believed it was clearly the constitutional obligation of Congress to provide the resources for victory.[107]

The similarity of Helms with Macon in respect to the question of principles and tactics is astonishing. Soon after taking his senatorial seat under a Republican president in 1973, Helms declared: "I was not sent here to serve a particular party or a particular administration or a particular President. I campaigned as a man loyal to certain principles and I was sent here to defend those principles."[108] In 1990 his proudest boast was that he had "not once... bent a principle."[109]

Indeed, again and again, the senator's supporters argue that he went to Washington to fight for principle, not for personal gain. Even someone not in sympathy with Helms's philosophy, Paul Luebke, wrote: "Senate financial reports uphold that faith in Helms. In 1988, he was among the least affluent of the one hundred senators--fellow Tar Heel Terry Sanford reported four times as much wealth."[110]

Helms has a firm understanding of senate rules which he has frequently utilized over the years by introducing amendments on such issues as abortion, busing, prayer in schools, AIDS funding, federally-funded art, etc. Helms's amendments have the intention of, noted one reporter, "forcing his colleagues to go on the record on all manner of questions that they would prefer to avoid." Many Helms amendments, because of their electoral popularity, have actually passed by large majorities to be killed by typical political chicanery in closed conference committees.[111]

Helms admired Reagan much as Macon admired Jefferson, but this admiration did not get in the way of his consistent philosophy. Helms, in fact, gained considerable notoriety during the Reagan administration for opposing diplomatic appointments on ideological grounds. He was critical of the State Department and "leftist" foreign policy. He did not always prevent certain appointments, but he always made his point and paved the way for his eventual chairmanship of the Senate Foreign Relations Committee.[112]

Hedrick Smith has argued that Helms represents "the power of obstruction, a negative power, the power to block and deny, the power of being difficult and prickly." Smith referred to this as "porcupine power."[113] Helms answered this argument when he defended Barry Goldwater decades ago against charges of being negative: "The most positive aspects of human development are often stated in the negative. The Ten Commandments, for example, consist largely of warnings to mankind that 'Thou shalt not...' The Bill of Rights devotes itself almost entirely to what the federal government shall not do. If these are 'negative' declarations, America could do with a great deal more negativism."[114]

The Politics of Personal Morality

      President John Tyler said of Macon: "Nothing sordid ever entered into his imagination;" while Macon's biographer, William E. Dodd, proclaimed that he "never knew vice."[115] What did they mean? Certainly, Macon drank corn whiskey at meals, a habit formed in youth, though Dodd states that "he regretted his appetite for drink." He raced horses, fox hunted, and was known to play cards. There is a legend that he even played cards for the hand of his future wife, Hannah Plummer.[116]

      Words frequently used to describe the character of Macon were "pure," "honest," and "sincere." The minor weaknesses that the man displayed did not detract from, but rather added luster to, those moral qualities that others saw in him. As Ingersoll said, Macon was "tenacious and inflexible, remonstrance availed nothing with him."[117] But he nonetheless rose to position and influence because he was a man of "constant integrity." He was elected and reelected, argued Josephus Daniels, because the people of North Carolina "shared his political faith and knew him to be a fixed star."[118] It is therefore understandable that Zane L. Miller, writing about Macon in 1961, found it easy "to predict his stand on most of the issues with which he was confronted. Senator Macon proved to be a remarkably consistent man."[119]

The same can be said with equal validity of Senator Helms. A "typical" politician can easily modify his position overnight. In contrast, there is in Helms, as President Tyler said of Macon, "a beautiful consistency." No man ever lost a night's sleep for fear that Helms would shift his position. "As a believing Christian," wrote Helms, "I do not resort to the dodge of having one set of principles for public issues and another for my personal use."[120] To Helms there is no logical disconnect between private morality and public ethics, and one cannot practice moral relativism on the one hand and then expect "the most ethical administration in the history of the Republic."[121]

Helms's basic principles, like Macon's, are so well understood that a majority of voters can predict with relative certainty how he will vote on a given issue. Compromise is the life blood of the typical politician, but it flows not in the veins of Senator Helms. In a very real sense this makes Helms the anti-politician. No matter how long he remains in Washington he will be able to say what he said in 1973 when a reporter suggested that senate insiders would make him into a moderate. "I'll continue to look at things as I always have," he responded.[122] And so he has.

One Man's Demagogue

A man of wealth and status, an elitist member of the establishment of his day, spoke to Josephus Daniels of Macon in 1884. He said, "He was a fine man, but he was a demagogue." Daniels responded that "a demagogue is one who plays an insincere role in public life for the sake of gaining political influence and office," and that by this definition Macon was clearly not a demagogue for he "personified sincerity."[123] To share the beliefs of one's neighbors and kinsmen, as Macon clearly did, and to militantly defend those beliefs was not demagoguery.

A similar argument as that presented by Daniels can be used in an evaluation of Helms. As a critic once said of the senator: "His certitude is such that he is in a class by himself. "It should come as no surprise, given his firm convictions, that a 1998 survey of congressional staffers voted Helms" the senator with the strongest backbone."[124] Helms has been accused of many things, but insincerity is not one of them. In fact, most of his opponents are against him for the opposite reason--they fear that he means what he says.

Most, however, misunderstand what Helms means, wrongly viewing him as one who wishes to force others to conform to his vision of America. In truth, if the senator were to have his idea of a perfect federal government, it would be far smaller and less obtrusive than currently. He would agree with Macon who felt that the average citizen if left alone "would continue to raise boys and girls who would become men and women. These were the sorts of internal improvements he desired to see."[125] Under Helms's conception North Carolina and Massachusetts would both have "room for the organic development of local traditions and interests."[126] Senator Helms holds a very traditional Southern view of the primacy of local and state interests. For obvious reasons this arrangement would be unacceptable to those who believe in federal intervention in the South.

Helms's traditionalist convictions are often unyielding, though scarcely classifiable as demagoguery. At a time when the number of politicians who posture based on poll results and focus groups is legion, Senator Helms certainly stands out. Indeed, many prominent individuals, having made a career out of public insincerity and lack of conviction, have risen to notably high office. Such persons would, by the Daniels definition, be the true demagogues of our age.

Makers
of Revolutions

Today most people do not realize that there was strong opposition to Thomas Jefferson for president in 1800. Many considered him too "radical" to be a national leader. The Federalist party, which controlled every branch of the federal government and a significant number of states, did not relinquish power easily. Macon used his influence for Jefferson in North Carolina. Even with this, there developed a tie between Jefferson and Aaron Burr, the Republican vice presidential nominee. The election was thrown into the House of Representatives where it took thirty-six ballots to elect. The Republican takeover of government was called "The Revolution of 1800." Jefferson immediately gave Macon control of patronage in North Carolina and Congress elected him Speaker of the House. Macon, in 1803, cast the deciding vote on the Twelfth Amendment which provided for separate electoral balloting for president and vice president thus preventing a recurrence of the 1800 election dispute.[127]

Who is father of the congressional Republican majorities of 1994 and 1996? A recent book on Newt Gingrich carries the inflated subtitle "Leader of the Second American Revolution," while Gingrich's own book, To Renew America, reveals as much reliance on futurists and science fiction authors as on traditional conservative thinkers.[128] Long before Gingrich was in Congress, Helms alone cried out in the wilderness.

In 1976 Helms broke rank with the establishment to support Ronald Reagan for president against incumbent Gerald Ford. A series of defeats for the ex-governor of California led Ford strategists to conclude that Reagan was finished. Then on March 23, with the backing of Helms, Reagan upset political prognosticators by winning the North Carolina primary. Rowland Evans and Robert Novak wrote: "Without his North Carolina victory, Ronald Reagan at sixty-five would surely have drifted into political oblivion."[129] Michael Barone's well-respected <u>Almanac of American Politics</u> concluded about the Reagan victory: "What would history have done without North Carolina?"[130] Indeed, what would history have done without Jesse Helms? It was only just before the primary that, at Helms's urging, Reagan switched to strong conservative themes. Without the Reagan '80s there would have been no resurgent Reaganism in the 1990s,[131] and Americans would never have heard a president produced by 1960's radicalism proclaim, "The era of big government is over."[132]

Conclusion: Heirs of "Pure Republicanism"

Writing of North Carolinians in 1905, Samuel A. Ashe said: "They have ever been conservative in their ideas and political action."[133] Macon was the premier early representative of the Tar Heel state's conservative character and as such set a pattern for subsequent conservative politicians, especially in his home state.[134]

Henry Adams, writing in the late nineteenth century, found that in North Carolina "the best qualities of the State were typified in its favorite representative, Nathaniel Macon."[135] Josephus Daniels goes further: "Macon was the highest product of North Carolina's hopes, North Carolina's faith, North Carolina virtues and provincialisms.... [William A.] Graham would have fitted into the life of Pennsylvania, [George E.] Badger would have shown in Boston, but you could not think of Macon in any other but a North Carolina rural environment."[136]

In evaluating Macon, Jefferson believed him to be "the strictest of our models of genuine republicanism.... 'Ultimus Romanorum.'" He personally commended Macon for his efforts to stop those wishing "to transfer all to Washington."[137] The worldly wise

Jefferson was wise enough to recognize that Macon's qualities, and not his own, were those of a genuine Republican "man of the people."

By the late 1840s a Pennsylvanian could observe that "the influence of his [Macon's] example is still enduring and increasing" and that "his doctrine already affects all our institutions."[138] But, in less than a generation, his memory was washed away in the blood of civil war and Henry Adams wrote: "No man in America left a better name than Macon; but the name was all he left."[139]

Is that true? In 1906 historian William E. Dodd believed that Macon's "impress upon North Carolinians has not yet been effaced. His traits became in a large measure theirs."[140] Senator Helms as recently as 1982 said: "All North Carolinians should be proud of Nathaniel Macon, and revere his memory."[141] The traits of the old "negative radical" abide still. Helms, born in 1921, was raised in a typical small Southern town. The same independent and provincial spirit that nurtured the young Macon still had power in such a town in the 1920s and 1930s. It is no wonder that Helms's favorite Jeffersonian adage is that "the <u>least</u> government is the <u>best</u> government."[142]

Sam Ervin, who often disagreed with Helms, nevertheless saw him as "one of the few men in public life who's got the courage to stand up for what he honestly believes. Courage is the rarest trait among public men. Many of them are intelligent, but there are very few of them that are courageous." George Bush viewed Helms as "a man who embodies the values of North Carolina's quiet and decent people--God-fearing good citizens..."[143]

Helms, like Macon, is the exemplary and unique product of North Carolina; and as with Macon, it is hard to imagine him emerging from any other than a rural Tar Heel environment. Unlike the state's more liberal politicians, many of whom represent a merging of North Carolina conceptions with outside influences,[144] Helms is pure Tar Heel. Gentlemanly in his personal relations, devout in his faith, uncompromising in his principles, lacking in TV-age "charisma," and viewing government as a necessary evil, Helms stands out as the ultimate anti-politician of the era.

Despite the dramatic demographic changes in North Carolina during the past three decades there is a continued dynamism in the state's older political traditions as represented by Helms. Indeed, Luebke reluctantly acknowledges not only the state, but the national impact of Helms, whom he feels has "pulled the political agenda to the right...." In a laudatory article Fred Barnes, executive editor of The Weekly Standard, refers to Helms as "the most inner-directed person in Washington" and adds: "No conservative, save Reagan, comes close to matching Helms's influence on American politics and policy in the quarter-century since he won a Senate seat in North Carolina."[145] Nationally, more and more persons are migrating to Helms's position. Given the senator's religious convictions, it is notable that a recent analysis by Albert J. Menendez has concluded that the more religious persons are also the more politically conservative. Voting based on religious perceptions has been increasing since the 1960s.[146]

In the final analysis, Helms represents the nationalization of a major political tradition of his home state. He himself wrote in 1988: "North Carolina has played a key role in the modern conservative movement. It will be pivotal in the years ahead." He continued, expressing a Maconian faith in the American people: "Liberals have indeed captured the minds of the powerful, but they will never win the hearts of the people."[147]

Economic determinists may continue to explain both Macon and Helms in class terms. For them it is no doubt more uncomfortable to consider the broader implications posed by the fact that Senator Helms, the inheritor of the Macon legacy, has maintained a national following for twenty-five years. This alone is strong evidence that an old and tested strain of Southern conservatism still resonates with many beyond the geographic boundaries of the Tar Heel state. Helms has always maintained that he is a defender of a uniquely American tradition. His numerous parallels both philosophically and operationally to Senator Nathaniel Macon support that contention.

View of the Capitol building after its destruction by the British in 1814, while Macon was a member of Congress. From Development of the United States Capital (Washington: Government Printing Office, 1930), p. 14.

View of the Capitol building after its restoration in 1827, as it would have appeared during Macon's last year as a Senator. From Development of the United States Capital (Washington: Government Printing Office, 1930), p. 21.

Macon allowed no portraits of himself in his lifetime and this likeness is based on a painting that was done after his death.

The isolated grave of Nathaniel Macon, located in rural Warren County, North Carolina, is a site visited by Senator Helms.

Washington 7 Feby 1819

Sir

I have in my seat this minute received your letter of the 3. instant; you ask my opinion concerning the conduct of Genl Jackson in the Seminole war; and inform me that you have formed yours, but will not give it. the example does not agree with the request; notwithstanding this; I shall state mine. the constitution gives congress the sole authority to declare war; war has been waged and every act of sovereign power exercised without the consent of Congress — the constitution has then been violated, and I am for the constitution rather than for man; no more for want of time at present

y.rs with esteem

Nathl Macon

Washington 26 Dec. 1824

Sir

From conversation with General Lafayette yesterday, I imagine he will be in North Carolina, much sooner than I expected, when I wrote you about his extended visit to the State. Perhaps it would be advisable to have all things in readiness to receive him; that is to be minute men for the occasion

I am very respectfully
Sir
Y. ob.t. Ser.
Na. H. Macon

N.B. The General told me, he wished to visit the southern & western States, & be at Boston by the 10 of June &c.

NOTES

1. John C. Calhoun, <u>The Papers of John C. Calhoun</u>, 23 vols., ed. by Clyde N. Wilson (Columbia: University of South Carolina, 1959-96) 10:194. Clyde Wilson, editor of the Calhoun Papers, identifies an open letter from "Patrick Henry," 8 August 1826, as being authored by President John Quincy Adams.

2. Charles J. Ingersoll, <u>Historical Sketch of the Second War Between the United States and Great Britain</u>, 2 vols. (Philadelphia: Lea and Blanchard, 1845-49), 1:211.

3. William E. Dodd, <u>Life of Nathaniel Macon</u> (New York: Burt Franklin, 1970), 22; Clarence Poe, "Nathaniel Macon, Cincinnatus of America," <u>South Atlantic Quarterly</u> 37 (January 1938):12.

4. J. G. DeRoulhac Hamilton, "Nathaniel Macon," <u>Dictionary of American Biography</u>, 20 vols. (New York: Charles Scribner's Sons, 1933), 12:158. See also Clyde N. Wilson, "Nathaniel Macon," <u>Dictionary of North Carolina Biography</u>, 6 vols. ed. by William S. Powell (Chapel Hill: University of North Carolina Press, 1979-1996), 4:185.

5. Thomas Pittman, "Nathaniel Macon" [July 4, 1902] <u>Literary and Historical Activities of North Carolina, 1900-1905</u> (Raleigh: E. M. Uzzle, 1907), 304. Pittman attributes this quotation to "a recent North Carolina publication," but it is striking for its similarity to Henry Adams's description of Macon as "a typical homespun planter, honest and

simple, erring more often in his grammar and spelling than in his moral principles."
See Henry Adams, <u>History of the United States...</u>, 9 vols. (New York: Antiquarian Press
Ltd., 1962) 1:267.

6. Ernest B. Furgurson, <u>Hard Right: The Rise of Jesse Helms</u> (New York: W. W. Norton
& Co., 1986), 25.

7. Elizabeth Drew, " Reporter at Large: Jesse Helms," <u>New Yorker</u> 57 (July 20, 1981):78.

8. Paul Luebke, <u>Tar Heel Politics: Myths and Realities</u> (Chapel Hill: University of
North Carolina Press, 1990), 18.

9. Luebke, <u>Tar Heel Politics</u>, 1-27. Luebke's analysis was influenced by both V.O. Key
Jr.'s study <u>Southern Politics in State and Nation</u> (New York: Random House, 1949) and
Dwight B. Billings Jr.'s study <u>Planters and the Making of the "New South": Class,
Politics, and Development in North Carolina, 1865-1900</u> (Chapel Hill: University of
North Carolina Press, 1979).

10. Stephen J. Barry, "Nathaniel Macon: Prophet of Pure Republicanism, 1758-1837,"
(PhD Dissertation, State University of New York at Buffalo, 1996), vii.

11. Christopher M. Duncan, <u>The Anti-Federalists and Early American Political Thought</u>
(DeKalb, Illinois: Northern Illinois University Press, 1995), 129, 132-133, 145. On page
133 Duncan writes: "The genius of the Federalists as politicians was their ability to
usurp the agenda-setting power of their opponents and make it appear that Anti-
Federalist thought was something new that arose in reaction to that of the Federalists,
when in reality it was the other way around." James H. Broussard's study of the
Federalist party reveals that while the Federalists were stronger in NC than any other
Southern state they were still far weaker than their Republican opposition: "North

Carolina Federalists, 1800-1816," <u>North Carolina Historical Review</u> 55 (January 1978): 18-41, and <u>Southern Federalists, 1800-1816</u> (Baton Rouge, LA: LSU Press, 1978), 215-234.

12. Thomas Hart Benton, <u>Thirty Years View</u>, 2 vols. (New York: D. Appleton & Co., 1886), 1:114, 118.

13. Barry, "Nathaniel Macon," 26.

14. Jesse Helms, Conversation with Ronnie W. Faulkner, Campbell University, Buies Creek, North Carolina, 27 August 1996; Helms to Faulkner, 4 November 1997, letter in possession of author.

15. Dodd, <u>Life of Nathaniel Macon</u>, 9.

16. Barry, "Nathaniel Macon," 170.

17. Dodd, <u>Nathaniel Macon</u>, 9, 23-30; Benton, <u>Thirty Years View</u>, 1:114-118.

18. Shawn Bonath, <u>Buck Spring Plantation: Archeology of an Old South Plantation in Warren County, North Carolina</u> (Raleigh: Division of Archives and History, 1978), 4.

19. Macon to John Randolph, 6 March 1829, Elizabeth G. McPherson, "Letters from Nathaniel Macon to John Randolph of Roanoke," <u>North Carolina Historical Review</u> 38 (October 1962): 665.

20. Frank L. Owsley, <u>Plain Folk of the Old South</u> (Baton Rouge: Louisiana State University Press, 1982, c1949). M. E. Bradford wrote in <u>Remembering Who We Are: Observations of a Southern Conservative</u> (Athens: University of Georgia Press, 1985), 56-57: "No work of scholarship in American history more disturbs the Marxist or 'New Left' intellectual community. For the burden of Owsley's analysis is that the patriarchal

culture of the antebellum South knew the secret of maintaining flexible but distinctive social classes and a various distribution of property without exposure to the perils of class struggle."

21. Furgurson, <u>Hard Right</u>, 43.

22. <u>Biographical Directory of the United States Congress, 1774-1989</u> (Washington, D.C.: Government Printing Office, 1989), 1168; "Helms, Jesse A.," <u>Current Biography 1979</u>, ed. by Charles Moritz (New York: H.W. Wilson, 1979), 165-167.

23. Luebke, <u>Tar Heel Politics</u>, 150-153; William D. Snider, <u>Helms and Hunt: The North Carolina Senate Race, 1984</u> (Chapel Hill: University of North Carolina Press, 1985), 215.

24. Alexis de Tocqueville, <u>Democracy in America</u>, George Lawrence, trans. (Garden City, N.Y.: Doubleday Anchor Books, 1969), 292-293. Helms is a great admirer of Tocqueville. See his WRAL-TV Viewpoint 2495, 7 January 1971, Rare Book Collection, Library, Campbell University, Buies Creek, North Carolina, and also his book <u>When Free Men Shall Stand</u> (Grand Rapids, MI: Zondervon, 1976), 54. A revised edition of this book was published in 1994 by Potomac Publishing, and whenever that edition is used hereafter the date will be given to distinguish it from the original edition.

25. Poe, "Nathaniel Macon," 20; Dodd, <u>Life of Nathaniel Macon</u>, 376-377.

26. [William K. Boyd], "Nathaniel Macon in National Legislation," <u>Trinity College Historical Society Papers</u> 4 (1900):74.

27. Macon to Bartlett Yancey, 1821, cited in Pittman, "Nathaniel Macon," 296.

28. Macon to Bartlett Yancey, 12 December 1823, "Nathaniel Macon and Bartlett Yancey," <u>The University Magazine</u>, 7 (October 1857):97.

29. Macon to Joseph H. Nicholson, 28 February 1809, cited in Barry, "Nathaniel Macon," 129.

30. Macon to Bartlett Yancey, 15 April 1818, "Nathaniel Macon and Bartlett Yancey," 95-96.

31. Josephus Daniels, "Daniels Lauds Democratic Principles of Nathaniel Macon," Raleigh <u>News and Observer</u>, 29 May 1935; Barry in his 1996 dissertation (p. 27) sees a clear correlation between Macon's religious and political views: "His later reliance on the Constitution, for instance, may very well have been influenced by his reading of the Bible. Furthermore, his strict adherence to the very letter of constitutional law seems to correspond to his attempts to strictly adhere to his religious faith."

32. Ferrel Guillory, "The Right Hand of God: Jesse Helms's Political Theology," <u>Commonweal</u> 122 (January 27, 1995): 4. See also Guillory, "A Political Paradox: North Carolina's Twenty-Five Years Under Jim Hunt and Jesse Helms," <u>Southern Cultures</u> 4 (Spring 1998): 52-61.

33. Helms, <u>When Free Men Shall Stand</u>, 15-16.

34. Hugh T. Lefler, <u>North Carolina History Told by Contemporaries</u> (Chapel Hill: University of North Carolina Press, 1956), 141; Dodd, <u>Life of Nathaniel Macon</u>, 117, 137-138.

35. <u>North Carolina Government, 1585-1974: A Narrative and Statistical History</u>, ed. by John L. Cheney (Raleigh: North Carolina Department of Secretary of State, 1975), 814-815, 822. See M. Stanton Evans, "The Christian History of the U.S. Constitution," <u>Human Events</u>, 59 (April 19, 1996):12-13, and Leonard W. Levy, <u>The Establishment Clause:</u>

Religion and the First Amendment, 2nd Rev. Ed. (Chapel Hill: University of North Carolina Press, 1994), 52-54.

36. Proceedings and Debates of the Convention of North Carolina... Raleigh, June 4, 1835 (Raleigh: J. Gales and Son, 1836), 246-248.

37. Cheney, North Carolina Government, 841, 861; Dodd, Life of Nathaniel Macon, 389.

38. Helms, When Free Men Shall Stand, 19, 21, 122.

39. M. E. Bradford, Original Intentions: On Making and Ratification of the United States Constitution (Athens: University of Georgia Press, 1993), 99.

40. M. Stanton Evans, The Theme is Freedom: Religion, Politics, and the American Tradition (Washington, DC: Regnery Publishing, Inc., 1994), 307. See also Evans, "The Christian History of the U.S. Constitution," 12-13.

41. Robert H. Bork, Slouching Towards Gomorrah: Modern Liberalism and American Decline (New York: HarperCollins, 1996), 272-295, 336-337.

42. Macon to Joseph H. Nicholson, 28 April 1810, "Macon Papers," ed. by William E. Dodd, The John P. Branch Historical Papers of Randolph-Macon College, 3 (June 1909): 63.

43. Annals of Congress, 16th Cong. 1st Sess., 231.

44. Macon quoted in Pittman, "Nathaniel Macon," 301; Barry, "Nathaniel Macon," 184.

45. Robert H. Bork, The Tempting of America: The Political Seduction of the Law (New York: The Free Press, 1990), 143-160, 164-165.

46. <u>Congressional Record</u>, 93rd Cong. 1st Sess., 29033; Helms, <u>When Free Men Shall Stand</u>, 25, (1994), 98.

47. Charles Evans Hughes, <u>Addresses and Papers of Charles Evans Hughes, 1906-1908</u> (New York: G.P. Putnams, 1908), 139.

48. Dodd, <u>Life of Nathaniel Macon</u>, 416, 427. Macon's entire speech on the Judiciary Act, 23 February 1802, is printed in an Appendix on pages 404-429.

49. Macon to John Steele, 11 June 1803, <u>Letters of Nathaniel Macon, John Steele and William Berry Grove, with Sketches and Notes by Kemp P. Battle</u> (Chapel Hill: University of North Carolina Press, 1902), 36-37.

50. Jefferson to Macon, 19 August, 20 October 1821, <u>The Writings of Thomas Jefferson</u>, ed. by Paul L. Ford (New York: G. P. Putnams, 1892-1899), 10:192, 194.

51. Ingersoll, <u>Historical Sketch of the Second War...</u>, 1:210.

52. Jesse Helms, WRAL-TV Viewpoint 2096, 20 May 1969. See also Viewpoint 2098, 22 May 1969.

53. Helms, <u>When Free Men Shall Stand</u> (1994), 99.

54. M. E. Bradford, <u>Original Intentions</u>, 71-86, makes a strong case about the religious nature of the country's founders. When the issue of the Supreme Court's powers came up at the North Carolina Ratification Convention in July of 1788, even the Federalist supporters of the Constitution argued from a decentralized state's rights position. Federalist William Richardson Davie said, "There is no instance that can be pointed out wherein the internal policy of the state can be affected by the judiciary of the United

States."(p. 76) Both sides argued from premises that would be perfectly comprehensible to Helms.

55. Macon to Crawford, 13 October 1817, "Macon Papers," 75.

56. Annals of Congress, 18th Cong. 1st Sess., 401.

57. James M. Helms, Jr., "The Early Career of Nathaniel Macon: A Study in 'Pure Republicanism,'" (PhD Dissertation, University of Virginia, 1962), 56-57.

58. Dodd, Life of Nathaniel Macon, 75; Helms, "The Early Career of Nathaniel Macon," 25-26.

59. Robert C. Byrd, The Senate, 1789-1989: Addresses on the History of the United States Senate, 4 vols. (Washington, DC: Government Printing Office, 1989-1994), 1:85; Dumas Malone, Jefferson and His Times, 6 vols. (Boston: Little, Brown, 1948-1977), 6:178.

60. Annals of Congress, 9th Cong. 1st Sess., 703.

61. Macon to Willie P. Mangum, 14 January 1827, The Papers of Willie P. Mangum, ed. by Henry T. Shanks, 3 vols. (Raleigh: State Department of Archives and History, 1950-1956), 1:306.

62. Annals of Congress, 6th Cong. 1st Sess., 282.

63. Macon to Bartlett Yancey, 24 December 1924, Letters of Nathaniel Macon..., 83.

64. Benton, Thirty Years View, 1:118; Helms, "The Early Career of Nathaniel Macon," 69-70; Barry, "Nathaniel Macon," 175-176; Adams, History of the United States..., 119-

122, 135-138, 144-146; <u>Annals of Congress,</u> 14th Cong. 1st Sess., 190, 193. While Macon voted against the raise, he did accept payment of the new salary until the repeal was enacted.

65. <u>Congressional Record</u>, 97th Cong. 2nd Sess., 31605.

66. Helms, <u>When Free Men Shall Stand</u>, 49, (1994) 63.

67. Helms, <u>When Free Men Shall Stand</u> (1994), 72.

68. George Bush, <u>Public Papers of the Presidents of the United States, 1990</u>, 2 vols. (Washington, DC: Government Printing Office, 1991), 2:1389; "Helms Asks Salary Cut," Raleigh <u>News and Observer</u>, 12 February 1976.

69. Pittman, "Nathaniel Macon," 301.

70. <u>Annals of Congress</u>, 9th Cong. 1st Sess., 386; 16th Cong. 1st Sess., 223.

71. Dodd, <u>Life of Nathaniel Macon</u>, 409.

72. <u>Annals of Congress</u>, 5th Cong. 2nd Sess., 661; 16th Cong. 1st Sess., 361.

73. <u>Annals of Congress</u>, 16th Cong., 1st Sess., 226; Byrd, <u>The Senate</u>, 1:74.

74. Macon to John Randolph, 26 April 1829, Elizabeth G. McPherson, "Letters from Nathaniel Macon to John Randolph of Roanoke, <u>North Carolina Historical Review</u>, 39 (April 1961):206. Of course, Macon's concern for his slaves while he was living must be contrasted with the provision in his will permitting slave families to be broken up if "necessary." Because of the death of both his daughters and one son-in-law Macon was directly responsible for eleven grandchildren in his final years. Not being a rich

man, he was especially concerned with their economic fate at his death. This could explain his willingness to permit slave families to be separated in his will (See Barry, "Nathaniel Macon," 272-274).

75. <u>Annals of Congress</u>, 18th Cong. 1st Sess., 400.

76. Ingersoll, <u>Historical Sketch of the Second War</u>..., 1:213.

77. Helms, <u>When Free Men Shall Stand</u>, 26.

78. "Why North Carolina Said 'Yes' to Senator 'No,'" Raleigh <u>News and Observer</u>, 19 November 1978; Alan Crawford, <u>Thunder on the Right: The 'New Right' and the Politics of Resentment</u> (New York: Pantheon Books, 1980), 131.

79. "No Means No: Helms Cites North Carolina Precedent," <u>The Hill</u>, April 22, 1998; "Under the Dome," Raleigh <u>News and Observer</u>, May 3, 1998. See also Andrew Phillips, "The Rising Force on the Right: Jesse Helms Flexes His Conservative Muscle," <u>Maclean's</u> 110 (September 1, 1997): 36-39, which notes how the Helms Center in Wingate, North Carolina, emphasizes Jesse Helms's "Senator No" reputation.

80. <u>Annals of Congress</u>, 13th Cong., 2nd Sess., 1787.

81. Macon to Martin Van Buren, 1 January 1837, Nathaniel Macon Papers, North Carolina Division of Archives and History, Raleigh, North Carolina.

82. Barry, "Nathaniel Macon," 176-179.

83. Ron Paul and Lewis Lehrman, <u>The Case for Gold: A Minority Report of the U.S. Gold Commission</u> (Washington, D.C.: Cato Institute, 1982), ii.

84. Helms, <u>When Free Men Shall Stand</u>, 61-62.

85. <u>Annals of Congress</u>, 4th Cong. 2nd Sess., 1819-1820.

86. <u>Annals of Congress</u>, 14th Cong. 2nd Sess., 177-179.

87. <u>Annals of Congress</u>, 9th Cong. 1st Sess., 690, 703.

88. Macon to Thomas Jefferson, 21 May 1824, "Macon Papers," 83-84.

89. Macon to Bartlett Yancey, 15 April 1818, "Nathaniel Macon and Bartlett Yancey," 96.

90. Ingersoll, <u>Historical Sketch of the Second War</u>..., 1:212.

91. Benton, <u>Thirty Years View</u>, 1:118.

92. Helms, <u>When Free Men Shall Stand</u> (1994), 54.

93. <u>Congressional Quarterly Almanac, 96th Cong., 1st Sess... 1979</u> (Washington, D.C.: CQ, Inc. 1980), 16C, 82S; Luebke, <u>Tar Heel Politics</u>, 85-101; Crawford, <u>Thunder on the Right</u>, 131. For Helms's argument to lower tobacco price supports see <u>Congressional Record</u>, 99th Cong. 1st Sess., 31930-31931. The reason Helms's general support of tobacco stands out so sharply and is so often brought up by critics is that inconsistencies of any kind are so rare in the senator's long career that opponents are often forced to grasp for straws.

94. Jesse Helms, WRAL-TV Viewpoint 2488, 29 December 1970; 2761, 17 February 1972.

95. Furgurson, <u>Hard Right</u>, 74-76.

96. Macon to Andrew Jackson, 26 August 1833, "Some Unpublished Letters of

Nathaniel Macon," ed. by John S. Bassett, <u>Trinity College Historical Society Papers</u> 6 (1906): 63.

97. Macon to Albert Gallatin, 13 February 1834, Henry Adams, <u>The Life of Albert Gallatin</u> (New York: Peter Smith, 1943), 596.

98. Helms, "The Early Career of Nathaniel Macon," 92-93.

99. <u>Annals of Congress</u>, 3rd Cong. 1st Sess., 648-651; Helms, "The Early Career of Nathaniel Macon," 40-41.

100. <u>Annals of Congress</u>, 5th Cong. 2nd Sess., 1111-1112.

101. <u>Annals of Congress</u>, 5th Cong. 2nd Sess., 1506.

102. <u>Annals of Congress</u>, 5th Cong. 2nd Sess., 1815-1816, 1825-1827; Dodd, <u>Life of Nathaniel Macon</u>, 118-120.

103. Helms, "The Early Career of Nathaniel Macon," 78.

104. Dodd, <u>Life of Nathaniel Macon</u>, 187.

105. <u>Annals of Congress</u>, 9th Cong. 1st Sess., 386.

106. <u>Annals of Congress</u>, 9th Cong. 1st Sess., 705.

107. Barry, "Nathaniel Macon," 150-153.

108. <u>Congressional Record</u>, 93rd Cong. 1st Sess., 14803.

109. Bush, <u>Public Papers... 1990</u>, 2:1390.

110. Luebke, <u>Tar Heel Politics</u>, 131.

111. Drew, "A Reporter At Large: Jesse Helms," 80; Charles Horner, "The Senator They Love to Hate," <u>Commentary</u> 93 (January 1992): 51-53.

112. Ernest B. Furgurson, "Ambassador Helms: At Home and Abroad, Right-Wing Leader Sen. Jesse Helms is a Force to be Reckoned With," <u>Common Cause Magazine</u>, 13 (March -April 1987): 16-21; Chistropher Madison, "Helms's Harangues: Sen. Jesse A. Helms is on the warpath against 'leftist' U.S. foreign policy," <u>National Journal</u> 18 (9 August 1986): 1948-1950.

113. Hedrick Smith, <u>The Power Game: How Washington Works</u> (New York: Random House, 1988), 58, 69.

114. Jesse Helms, WRAL-TV Viewpoint 2761, 17 February 1972.

115. Dodd, <u>Life of Nathaniel Macon</u>, 6; R. D. W. Connor, <u>Makers of North Carolina</u>, 2nd ed. (Raleigh: Alfred Williams & Co., 1930), 157. President John Tyler's full statement on Macon as quoted by Connor ran: "There was a beautiful consistency in his course, from the moment of his entering public life to the moment of his quitting it. Nothing sordid ever entered into his imagination. He was a devoted patriot whose whole heart and every corner of it was filled with love of country. In the House of Representatives he was the firm unflinching Republican, and in the Senate the venerable patriarch, contemporary of Washington and Franklin, and most worthy to have lived in the same century with them."

116. Dodd, <u>Life of Nathaniel Macon</u>, 302. 372; Daniels, "Nathaniel Macon," 82.

117. Ingersoll, <u>Historical Sketch of the Second War</u>..., 1: 212-213.

118. Daniels, "Nathaniel Macon," 82.

119. Zane L. Miller, "Senator Nathaniel Macon and the Public Domain, 1815-1828," <u>North Carolina Historical Review</u> 38 (October 1961): 485.

120. Helms, <u>When Free Men Shall Stand</u>, 67; Connor, <u>Makers of North Carolina</u>, 157. From the Helms perspective William Jefferson Clinton and his political shifting are perfect examples of what the senator abhors. Championing "values" and initially winning office with a sense of moral superiority over Ronald Reagan and the 1980s, Clinton's sixties-style moral relativism has spilled over into an administration plagued by scandals and indictments of numerous Clinton friends and officials.

121. Soon after election to the presidency Bill Clinton made the pledge about government ethical standards that has not been fulfilled in practice. See Tod Lindberg, "Morally Bankrupt Cronies of Clinton Rob Peter to Pay Paul," <u>Insight on the News</u> 11 (March 13, 1995): 40; Jamie Dettmer, "Clinton's Ethical Promises Are Proving Hard to Keep," <u>Insight on the News</u> 11 (April 17, 1995): 10-12: Bob Barr, "High Crimes and Misdemeanors: The Clinton-Gore Scandals and the Question of Impeachment," <u>Texas Review of Law and Politics</u> 2 (Fall 1997): 1-57, and Ann H. Coulter, <u>High Crimes and Misdemeanors: The Case Against Bill Clinton</u> (Washington D.C.: Regnery Publishing, 1998).

122. "Senator Jesse A. Helms, Jr.: North Carolina Interview," <u>North Carolina</u> (January 1973), 29-30, reprinted in <u>Congressional Record</u>, 93rd Cong. 1st Sess., 3521-3523. William Safire states in <u>Safire's Political Dictionary</u> (New York: Random House, 1978), 550: "...a <u>professional politician</u> (italics in original) is usually a technician without ideology." Unfortunately for modern political leaders, this is the way most people perceive politicians in general. A politician is considered to be practicing politics the more adept he is at compromising. Helms is an effective campaigner, but not an

effective compromiser. He does not practice politics in the conventional sense at all, and this makes him an "anti-politician" as that term is used above.

123. Josephus Daniels, "Nathaniel Macon, of Warren, 'The Last of the Romans,'" Raleigh News and Observer, 27 May 1923.

124. Drew, "Reporter At Large: Jesse Helms," 80; "Helms Wins D.C. Personality Contest, "Raleigh News and Observer, 20 July 1998.

125. Barry, "Nathaniel Macon," 297.

126. Congressional Record, 93rd Cong., 1st Sess., 29033. See William D. Snyder in Helms and Hunt, 214-215, for a typical view of Helms.

127. Barry, "Nathaniel Macon," 64-70; Dodd, Life of Nathaniel Macon, 156-167; Helms, "The Early Career of Nathaniel Macon," 273-278, 355-257; Malone, Jefferson and His Times, 3:459-506.

128. Dick Williams, Newt! Leader of the Second American Revolution (Marietta, GA: Longstreet Press, 1995); Newt Gingrich, To Renew America (New York: HarperCollins, 1995), 22, 52, 54, 190-191.

129. Rowland Evans and Robert Novak, The Reagan Revolution (New York: E. P. Dutton, 1981), 54; Lou Cannon, Reagan (New York: Putnam, 1982), 218.

130. Michael Barone and Grant Ujifusa, The Almanac of American Politics 1996 (Washington, D.C.: National Journal), 990. See also Jesse Helms, "Foreword," The Conservative Perspective: A View From North Carolina, ed. by Kevin Kennelly and Boyd Cathey (Charlotte: North Carolina Policy Council Press, 1988), 3.

131. David Keene, Chairman of the American Conservative Union, put it succinctly in a 1997 tribute to Helms: "Without Jesse Helms there'd have been no Reagan presidency." See "Remarks of David Keene at the Silver Anniversary Tribute to Jesse Helms," [July 22, 1997] (http://www.townhall.com/conservative/Helms.html). Fred Barnes even credits much of Ronald Reagan's success to Helms: "Reagan's success as a conservative leader... wouldn't have happened without Helms's bracing him." Barnes, "The Ascendancy of Jesse Helms," The Weekly Standard, 2 (August 11, 1997): 24.

132. William J. Clinton, "State of the Union 1996: The Age of Possibility," Vital Speeches of the Day 62 (February 15, 1996): 258.

133. Samuel A. Ashe, "The Story of the People," Biographical History of North Carolina From Colonial Times to the Present, 8 vols. (Greensboro: Charles L. Van Noppen, 1905-1917), 1:21.

134. Roy Thompson wrote in Before Liberty: Their New World Made North Carolinians Different (Lexington, NC: Piedmont Publishing, 1976): "Nathaniel Macon was a conservative if any man on the face of the earth ever deserved the name." See also Nobel E. Cunningham, Jr., "Nathaniel Macon and the Southern Protest Against National Consolidation," North Carolina Historical Review 32 (July 1955): 376-384.

135. Adams, History of the United States..., 1:148-149.

136. Daniels, "Nathaniel Macon," 84. William A. Graham (1804-1875), lawyer, planter, Whig governor, and North Carolina Unionist, was the Whig vice-presidential candidate in 1852. George E. Badger (1795-1866), judge, secretary of the navy, and Whig U.S. senator, was unsuccessfully nominated for the Supreme Court by President Millard Fillmore in 1853. Further information can be found in Lawrence London, "George

Edmund Badger," <u>Dictionary of North Carolina Biography</u>, 1:79-80 and Max Williams "William Alexander Graham," <u>Dictionary of North Carolina Biography</u>, 2:337-339.

137. Jefferson to Macon, 24 March 1826, quoted in Barry, "Nathaniel Macon," iv; Jefferson to Macon, 21 February 1826, Jefferson, <u>The Writings of Thomas Jefferson</u>, 10:378.

138. Ingersoll, <u>Historical Sketch of the Second War</u>..., 1:215, 217.

139. Adams, <u>History of the United States</u>..., 1:267.

140. Dodd, "Nathaniel Macon," <u>Biographical History of North Carolina</u>, 4:305.

141. <u>Congressional Record</u>, 97th Cong. 2nd Sess., 31605.

142. Jesse Helms, WRAL-TV Viewpoint 2285, 2 March 1970; 2184 2 October 1969.

143. Gene Marlowe, "Former Senator's [Sam Ervin's] View of President is Mixed," <u>Richmond Times-Dispatch,</u> 12 September 1982.

144. For example, Terry Sanford, one of the state's primary liberal politicians, long had close connections with the Kennedy family and the national Democratic Party. Too close a connection with the liberal policies and attitudes of the national party doubtless contributed to his defeat in the U.S. Senate race in 1992 when he was faced with strong conservative opposition from Lauch Faircloth. Similar associations led to the defeat of Senator Robert Morgan by John East in 1980. Both these victories followed the pattern established in Tar Heel senate races. See Carter Wrenn, "Recent Conservative Politics in North Carolina," <u>The Conservative Perspective: A View From North Carolina</u>, 53-62.

145. Luebke, <u>Tar Heel Politics</u>, 124-125; Barnes, "The Ascendancy of Jesse Helms," 19.

146. Albert J. Menendez, <u>Evangelicals at the Ballot Box</u> (Amherst, NY: Prometheus Books, 1996), 293-312. Menendez writes on p. 293: "There is abundant evidence that the U.S. political system is being transformed by religion.... Today's cultural divisions pit the conservative or orthodox adherents in all religions against the less conservative, or modernist, members of all religions.... Therefore, a fundamental realignment is developing in American public life, centered around different moral visions, concepts of authority, the nature of virtue, community, and the meaning of the American experience itself." Oran P. Smith's <u>The Rise of Baptist Republicanism</u> (New York: New York University Press, 1997), 191-212, provides strong evidence of the increasing political clout of Southern Baptists such as Helms. Interestingly enough, Southern Baptist conservatism is so strong that in both 1992 and 1996 Southern Baptists rejected the Clinton-Gore national ticket even though both men are Southern by birth and Baptist by affiliation.

147. Helms, "Foreword," <u>The Conservative Perspective</u>, 2-4.

About the Author

Dr. Ronnie W. Faulkner is a member of the Faculty of Campbell University where he serves as Director of Library Services and Associate Professor of History. His specialty is North Carolina history. Dr. Faulkner received his Bachelors degree from Campbell University, his Master of Arts in history from East Carolina University, his Master of Science in library science from the University of North Carolina at Chapel Hill and his Doctorate of Philosophy in history from the University of South Carolina. He is the author of a number of journal articles on history and political science, and his work has appeared in *The Historian*, the *North Carolina Historical Review,* the *Tennessee Historical Quarterly, Polity* and *Teaching Political Science*.

A native North Carolinian, Dr. Faulkner grew up watching Jesse Helms deliver WRAL-TV's Viewpoint editorials following the news each evening, even summoning the rest of the family to gather round when it was "time for Jesse." As a student of North Carolina's history, Dr. Faulkner studied the careers of both Senator Nathaniel Macon and Senator Jesse Helms. In Senator Helms's career Dr. Faulkner saw, not a departure from the traditions of North Carolina's history, but a return to the earliest traditions as exemplified by Senator Macon.

This ground-breaking book, Dr. Faulkner's first, points out the basic agrarian anti-federalism, strong religious faith, deep sense of personal morality, and opposition to big government that both men share(d). It also brings appropriate attention to their willingness to withstand criticism in the pursuit of their convictions.